HINDU

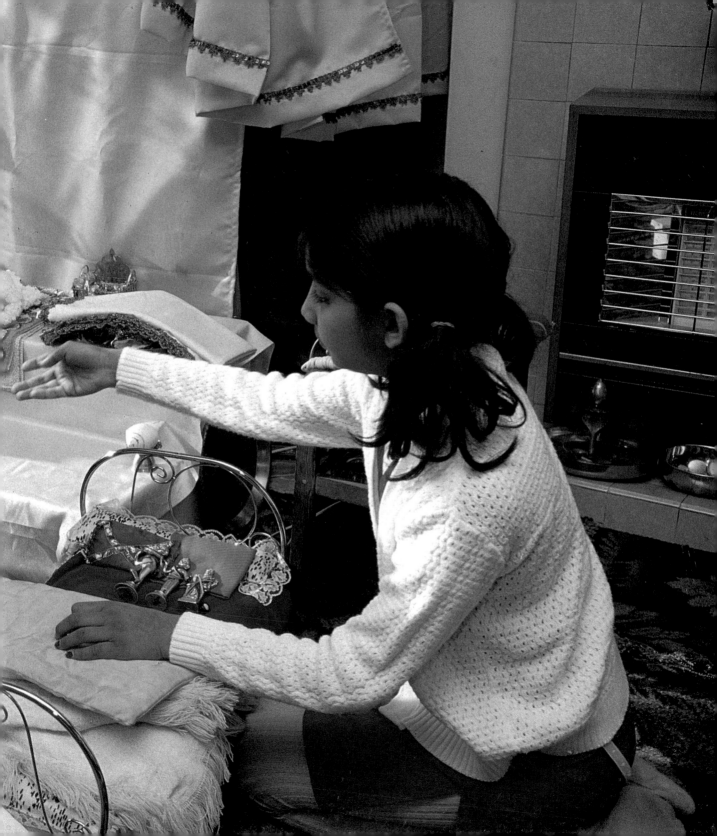

This edition 2003

Franklin Watts
96 Leonard Street
London
EC2A 4XD

Franklin Watts Australia
45-51 Huntley Street
Alexandria
NSW 2015

Design: Edward Kinsey
Typesetting: Tradespools Ltd

A CIP catalogue record for this book is available from the British Library.

Dewey decimal classification: 294.5

ISBN: 0 7496 5045 1

Printed in Italy

The publisher would like to thank the Goswami family and all other people shown in this book.

Note: Many of the photographs in this book originally appeared in 'My Belief: I am a Hindu'

Hindu

Jenny Wood

Photographs: Chris Fairclough
Consultant: A.T.S. Ratna Singham

W
FRANKLIN WATTS
LONDON•SYDNEY

These people are Hindus.
They follow the Hindu religion
which began in India
thousands of years ago.

Hindus believe there is
one great God, called Brahman.
There are also many other gods
that look like animals or humans.

Many Hindus have altars
in their homes.
Some have special rooms
where statues of the gods are kept.

Most Hindu men
wear European clothes.

Most Hindu women wear a long dress, called a sari. Many also wear a jewel in their nose, as well as bracelets and other jewellery.

This man is a Hindu priest.
The special sign
on his forehead shows
that he worships the god Krishna.

Before every meal,
he offers food to the gods.
This makes the food holy.

Hindu children learn the teachings of the Holy Books.

The Hindu Holy Books are written in a special script called Sanskrit.

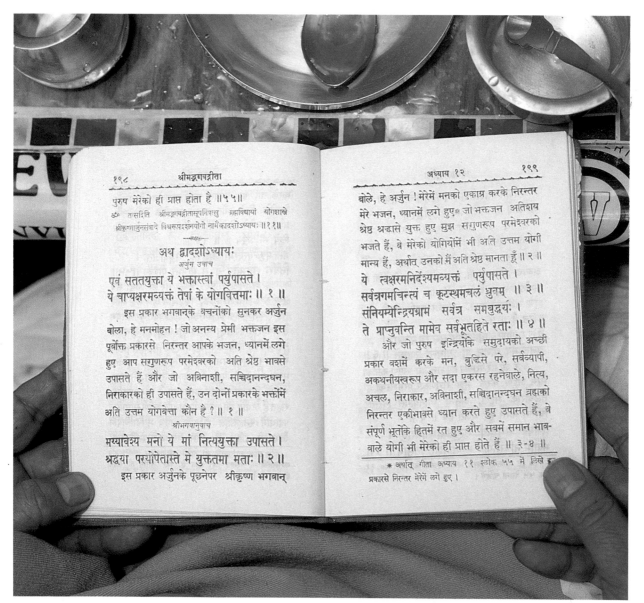

A Hindu temple is called a mandir.
Before going inside,
Hindus take off their shoes.
They say prayers
in front of a sacred flame.

The priest carries out
a special ceremony.
He moves a tray
with five candles
slowly in front of a god.

Most Hindus do not eat meat.
A favourite meal is vegetable curry
and a type of bread called puri.

Hindus have many rules about eating.
They must be clean
before they sit down for a meal.

A Hindu wedding ceremony takes place in the temple, under a special canopy.

The bride and groom take seven steps
around a sacred flame
to bless their marriage.
Their friends give them gifts
and wish them a happy life together.

After the ceremony, a meal is cooked in the temple kitchen.

Hindu festivals are happy occasions.
During Raksha Bandhan,
girls tie symbols called rakhis
on their brothers' wrists
in return for their protection.

Holi is the festival to celebrate
the start of spring.
Hindu children throw coloured powder
and water at each other.

Diwali is the festival of light.
There are firework displays,
and homes are lit
by lamps, candles and sparklers.

At the end of every day,
a Hindu family comes together
to pray and sing hymns.

FACTS ABOUT HINDUS

Hinduism is one of the oldest religions in the world. It began in India over 4,000 years ago.

Hindus believe that:
— the spirit of God is present in everything in the world — animals, plants and humans
— it is wrong to hurt any living thing
— a person has many lives and is reborn after death
— the way a person behaves during a lifetime will decide what their next life will be like
— a person has duties to their family and to God.

Hinduism divides people into social groups or castes.

Hinduism is the third largest religion in the world with over 500 million followers.

Most Hindus live in India, but they are also found in other parts of the world such as East Africa, Sri Lanka, Europe and North America.

In Britain there are about 300,000 Hindus. They came from East Africa, India and Pakistan.

GLOSSARY

Altar
A table or platform used for religious ceremonies.

Brahman
The Hindu word for God.

Diwali
The Hindu festival of light.

Holi
The Hindu festival which celebrates the start of spring.

Krishna
A Hindu god.

Mandir
A Hindu temple.

Raksha Bandhan
During this festival, a Hindu girl ties a symbol called a rakhi on a brother's wrist in return for his protection.

Sanskrit
The special script in which the Hindu Holy Books are written.

Sari
The traditional dress of Hindu women, made from one piece of cloth wound round the body.

INDEX

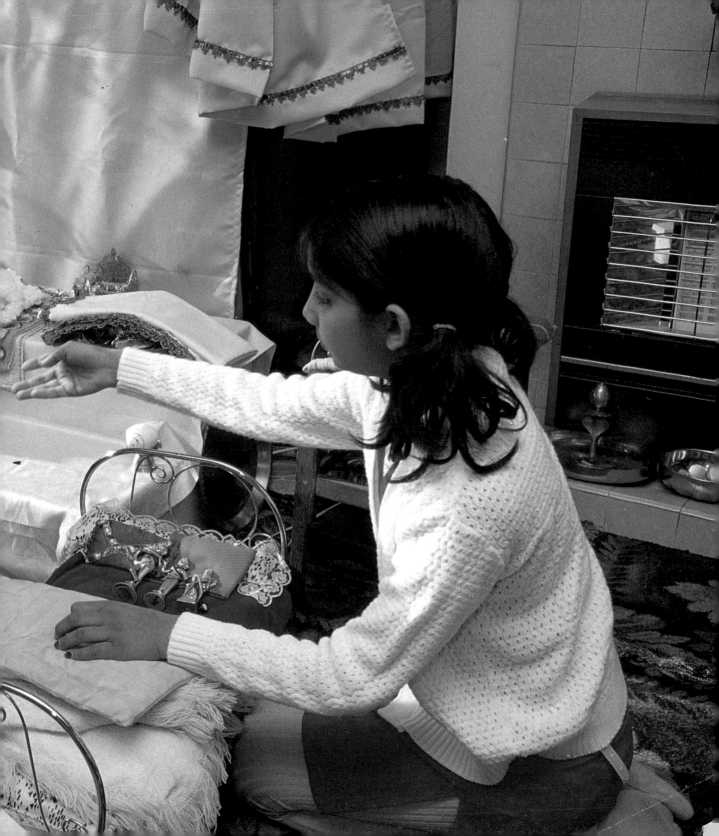